THE TRUTH ABOUT JESUS

by
John Redford

All booklets are published thanks to the generous support of the members of the Catholic Truth Society

CATHOLIC TRUTH SOCIETY
PUBLISHERS TO THE HOLY SEE

Contents

The truth about Jesus

Christianity has survived many attacks on it, from Roman Emperors in the first century to Nazi and Communist dictators in the twentieth. But one of the most bizarre attacks on its authenticity has come recently from what is in fact no more than a novel.

The *Da Vinci Code* is one of the best selling books of the new millennium. It is soon to be made into a movie, which will no doubt expand its huge audience still further. The book claims that the real story of Jesus is that he was married to Mary Magdalene, in the Gospels depicted as one of his disciples and who witnessed his resurrection from the dead. From Mary Magdalene Jesus had a child, it is claimed. The knowledge of this union, contrary to the "official" Christian story, was conveyed by secret code down the centuries, only to be discovered and finally revealed in the *Da Vinci Code*, two thousand years later.

It is claimed that the famous painter Leonardo Da Vinci knew of this Code, because in his painting of the Last Supper celebrated by Jesus and his disciples on the night of his arrest in the Garden of Gethsemane there appears to be a woman, whom Brown the author of the *Da Vinci Code* claims is Mary Magdalene. Art experts tend to think that it was another disciple of feminine aspect, since that is the way in which Da Vinci was accustomed to paint men. But Brown is convinced that it is Mary Magdalene, Jesus' "wife".

Some of my Catholic friends say to me, "There is no problem with this book. No one takes it seriously". Of course, those who have any systematic knowledge about Christian origins will see it for the nonsense it is. But I have heard other reactions. A close friend of mine, not a Catholic said, "John, I think that Jesus was married", as the *Da Vinci Code* claims. Others have said, "Well, the *Da Vinci Code* might be true, you never know."

I have written this pamphlet therefore for anyone who might think that any significant portion of the *Da Vinci Code* is actually proven historical fact. And my main aim is not to debunk what many find a rip-roaring read. It is to authenticate the true Jesus story, not written in any secret code, but available for all to see in our four Gospels, Matthew, Mark, Luke, and John; which have been read, preached, and believed by billions of people for two thousand years, as inspiration for this world, and as hope for the next.

Was Jesus married to Mary Magdalene?

There is no historical evidence whatsoever that Mary Magdalene was married to Jesus of Nazareth, still less that she bore a child by him.

The four Gospels are historically the earliest documents we possess about Jesus. All scholars agree on this; although they do not always give that historical fact the emphasis it deserves in their investigations. According to the general critical opinion, the first Gospel was compiled by Mark at about 64 B.C., Matthew and Luke about 80, and John the very latest 110 A.D.

That means that all four Gospels were compiled during the lifetime of those who knew Jesus, who was crucified some time between 26 and 36 A.D. This was the time span of the governorship in Jerusalem of Pontius Pilate, who condemned Jesus to death. Eye-witnesses could still have been alive to verify or falsify the events contained in the Gospels. You can hardly ask much more concerning the historical origin of ancient documents.

The Gospels do not say that Jesus was married to Mary Magdalene. On the contrary, they strongly imply the opposite. She is referred to as "Mary of Magdala" eleven times in the four Gospels[1], and once as "Mary Magdalene".[2] Strange that the Gospels do not say "Mary the wife of Jesus" if he was married to her! Karen King, who is a history professor at Harvard University and a leading authority on Mary Magdalene, says:-

> "The really odd thing would be to have Mary married to Jesus and have them next to each other in the same text, and for it not to be mentioned. That for me is quite conclusive that they were not married."[3]

Indeed it is. Mary of Magdala according to St John's Gospel was the first disciple to see her beloved Jesus risen from the dead.[4] Yet the Gospel does not mention that it was Jesus' own wife that saw him alive!

This is particularly strange because there would have been no problem theologically or morally for the writers of the four Gospels if Jesus *had* been married. Peter, made the chief disciple by Jesus, was married, as we are told in the Gospel.[5] Jesus healed miraculously his mother-in-law who lived in Capernaum. Emphasis on the teaching of virginity was a later development in the Church, with the growth of monasticism. Celibacy did not become obligatory for priests in the Western Church until the eleventh century.

St Paul, while unmarried himself, did not pressurize his newly converted Christians at Corinth, to whom he wrote his First Letter c.67 A.D., to take vows of celibacy. He left them entirely free, even though he presented the advantages of being unmarried in difficult times, so that the Corinthians would be "free from all worry".[6]

So, the first Christians were by no means fanatical propagandists for celibacy, but accepted equally the married state and the unmarried state as vocations from God. It would not concerned them in the slightest if Jesus had been married, even if as they claimed, he was the Son of God.

So why did the four Gospels keep it quiet? Simply because Jesus was *not* married, to Mary Magdalene or to anyone else. Jesus was of course a Jew, and most Jews married, as with most peoples. But we do have evidence of Jewish monks who took vows of celibacy at Qumran contemporary with the time of Jesus. And it is quite possible, for instance, that the prophet Jeremiah, who prophesied six centuries before Christ, was not married. In any civilization, some people choose not to marry, for one reason or another.

Jesus of Nazareth had good reason not to marry. He began his itinerant preaching and healing ministry at about thirty years of age. He went from town to town preaching the kingdom of God. The Gospels tell us that often he had no place to lay his head[7]. After perhaps three years preaching, he was arrested and charged by the Jewish Sanhedrin with blasphemy, because he claimed to be God.[8] He was aware for much of his life that he would suffer and die for his message.[9] Quite literally, there was no place in his life for a wife, to whom he would give only pain and mourning. It is quite likely that he was making an enigmatic reference to his own vocation when he said, according to the Gospel of Matthew:-

> "For there are eunuchs who have been so from birth, and there are eunuchs who have been made eunuchs by others, and there are eunuchs who have made themselves eunuchs for the sake of the kingdom of heaven. Let anyone accept this who can."[10]

Jesus is not referring to acts of self-mutilation, but to commitment to the kingdom of God, whereby a spiritual family is born, as he said: "Whoever does the will of God is my brother, and sister, and mother".[11] His family, his own brothers and sisters and mothers, now count billions. His is a family of faith, hope and love, not of blood-line.

It is not my purpose to catalogue all the historical falsities and errors in The *Da Vinci Code*; (leaving aside the question, of course, as to how much is intended to be fiction.) For this purpose, the CTS have produced another pamphlet. The reader is referred to that pamphlet to see how the whole idea of a "blood-line" through the Priory of Sion is total fabrication, going back only to 1950 A.D.!

Our purpose is rather to set out the true historical facts about Jesus. In the novel, Teabing tells the startled Sophie that in fact Mary Magdalene was made the leader of the Church, as well as that she was married to Jesus. These "facts" were "suppressed" by the anti-female Catholic Church.

This is far-fetched, even for fiction. For "evidence" that Jesus was married to Magdalene, Teabing pointed Sophie to the *The Gospel of Philip*, and for "evidence" that Jesus made Magdalene the head of the Church, he points Sophie to *The Gospel of Mary Magdalene*.[12] But, as we shall now see, these non-canonical Gospels give us no such information.

Gnosticism

Nag Hammadi

The Gospel of Philip and *The Gospel of Mary Magdalene* were part of a remarkable find near the town of Nag Hammadi in Upper Egypt in 1945 by a local inhabitant Muhammed Ali al-Samman.

Ali found a large collection of papyrus books bound in leather. It took some time before this discovery came to light, partly because they were released through the black market. But eventually these papyri were studied, and what emerged from investigation was a library of what we might call "alternative" Gospels, which presented a Gnostic Jesus. Gnosticism (from the Greek *gnosis* - "knowledge") was the New Age of the first three centuries A.D., which eventually was overcome by orthodox Christianity.

The date of these actual papyri is not in dispute. "Examination of the datable papyrus used to thicken the leather bindings, and the Coptic script, place them A.D. 350-400".[13] This is three hundred years at least after the time of Christ!

Scholars debate about how old the originals might have been. Certainly, there is evidence of opposition to Gnostic ideas in the writings of the great Catholic bishop Irenaeus of Lyons at the end of the second century. And Docetism[14] (the idea that the humanity of Christ was only apparent, a kind of Gnosticism) is even attacked in the First Letter of John, dated towards the end of the first century A.D.[15] John's readers are exhorted that they must believe that Jesus Christ truly came "in the flesh", i.e. he was truly human.

But even if we accept the possibility that these Gospels give authentic information about Jesus (which is at best purely hypothetical), *The Gospel of Philip* does not say that Jesus was married to Mary Magdalene, and *The Gospel of Mary Magdalene* does not say that Magdalene was made the leader of the Church by Jesus.

The passage from *The Gospel of Philip* which Teabing shows to Sophie[16] contains the following about Mary Magdalene and Jesus:-

> "And the companion of the Saviour is Mary Magdalene. Christ loved her more than all the disciples and used to kiss her often on her mouth. The rest of the disciples were offended by it and expressed disapproval. They said to him, 'Why do you love her more than all of these?"

Teabing says to Sophie, "As any Aramaic scholar will tell you, the word companion, in those days literally meant spouse".[17] But indeed, the scholars who have studied the texts in the original Coptic - not, as Teabing says, Aramaic, which was the language of Jesus, a Semitic language, but the Christian development of ancient Egyptian[18] - are by no means clear that "companion" in *The Gospel of Philip* means "spouse".

The word means much more generally "a person engaged in 'fellowship of sharing with someone or in something' not necessarily a spouse.[19] Interestingly enough, both Jean-Yves Leloup,[20] and Elaine Pagels,[21] who have studied closely the literature, and who are more sympathetic to Gnosticism than I would be, do not interpret this text as saying that Mary Magdalene was married to Jesus. Rather, they claim that their relationship was very close and spiritual. Similarly, the reference to Jesus kissing Mary Magdalene "on her mouth" would have the same meaning, that of "spiritual nourishment that leads to spiritual procreation, not an act of romantic love."[22]

In the same way, the text quoted by Teabing about Mary Magdalene as being made the leader of the Church by Jesus does not bear Teabing's interpretation of *The Gospel of Mary Magdalene*:-

> "And Peter said, 'Did the Saviour really speak with a woman without our knowledge? Are we to turn about and all listen to her? Did he prefer her to us?'
> And Levi answered, 'Peter, you have always been hot-tempered. Now I see you contending against the woman like an adversary. If the Saviour made her worthy, who are you indeed to reject her? Surely the Saviour knows her very well. That is why he loved her more than us.'"[23]

Why should the fact that Jesus loved Mary Magdalene more than the other disciples mean that he should make her the leader of his Church? In the Fourth canonical Gospel, the Gospel of John, Peter is clearly made the leader of the Church, being told by the risen Jesus "feed my sheep.[24] But who is "the disciple whom Jesus loved",[25] his greatest friend? Not Peter, but the beloved disciple himself, identified by Christian tradition with John the Son of Zebedee, the author of the Fourth Gospel.

A cynic would say that you would rather give the job of leadership to your greatest enemy than to the one you love the most. Such leadership, particularly for the early Church, was a road to martyrdom, as it was for Peter himself, and for most of the early Popes who succeeded him as Bishops of Rome.

Mary Magdalene, the Sacred Feminine?

The *Da Vinci Code* is a tease. After grisly murders, a chase by the Judicial Police by aeroplane to Biggin Hill Airport, a fight in London's Temple Church, a final journey north to Edinburgh to Rosslyn Chapel, do our heroes Robert and Sophie crack the *Da Vinci Code*?

Our couple go up to Rosslyn Chapel, and there are led to the Chapel Rectory, where they meet the curator Marie, who happens to be Sophie's long lost grandmother. After a tearful reunion, Marie takes them to the Chapel, where they expect to find the sacred symbols the blade and the chalice. Instead, they appear to see nothing, until they recognise the giant symbol of the Star of David.

This is not for Marie a post-biblical symbol of Jewish national identity (which it is in actual fact.[26]). No, for her it is the union of the male and female deity:-

> "The Star of David...the perfect union of male and female...Solomon's Seal...marking the Holy of Holies, where the male and female deities - Yahweh and Shekinah - were thought to dwell."[27]

Brown does not seem content simply to make Mary Magdalene the human wife of Jesus of Nazareth, who bore his child. Rather, does he not want us to think that the Magdalene is the feminine creative principle of the universe? In fact, is she not a goddess?

We might well think this when Brown brings his novel to an end. He makes Langdon have a kind of religious experience. Langdon expected to find the bones of Mary Magdalene in the Rosslyn Chapel. Instead, Langdon, kneeling at the place where the tomb of Mary Magdalene would have been had it existed, is grasped by the following ecstatic thought:-

> "For a moment, he thought he heard a woman's voice...the wisdom of the ages...whispering up from the chasms of the earth."[28]

Is this Mary Magdalene? Once more, we must remind ourselves, this is is a novel, not a religious treatise. But if Brown is seriously identifying Mary Magdalene as the sacred feminine herself, or even as a symbol of it, this seems to me to be heavy duty paganism. It was fiercely condemned long before the Catholic Church ever existed. It was condemned by the Hebrew prophets eight hundred years before Christ as an abominable perversion of true religion.

Holy, Holy, Holy

Readers of The *Da Vinci Code* must be prepared to be shocked. In the story, we are told that, at the time when he was murdered, Jacques Saunière had been estranged for many years from his granddaughter Sophie. She had been shocked by something she had seen him involved with.

We do not find out what that was until late into the narrative. What drove them apart was that when on vacation as a university student, Sophie had seen her grandfather involved in ritual sex. Far from confirming Sophie's natural revulsion, Langdon justified this "sacred" physical union. He insisted to Sophie, "Intercourse was the revered union of the two halves of the human spirit - male and female - through which the male could find spiritual wholeness and communion with God."[29]

But there is even more. Langdon claimed that:-

> "the early Jewish tradition involved ritualistic sex, *in the Temple, no less*". Early Jews believed that the Holy of Holies in Solomon's Temple housed not only God but also His powerful female equal Shekinah. Men seeking spiritual wholeness came to the Temple to

visit priestesses - or *hierodules* - with whom they made love and experienced the divine through physical union. The Jewish tetragrammaton YHWH - the sacred name of God - in fact derived from Jehovah, an androgynous physical union between the masculine *Jah* and the pre-Hebraic name for Eve, *Havah*".[30]

No wonder that Langdon found that his Jewish students "looked flabbergasted" when he told them this. Judaism would see this not only as heresy, but blasphemy. If you do not believe me, reader, go along to any Jewish rabbi and see what his reaction will be when you quote the above paragraph.

As usual, of course, Brown's scholarship is hopelessly awry. The Hebrew tetragrammaton (four-letter-word) YHWH occurs 6007 times in the Hebrew Bible. It is the sacred name of God, revealed to Moses on the "mountain of God".[31] It does not derive from a combination of *Jah* and *Havah*. On the contrary, the Book of Exodus, which in its final edited form dates back at least to the 5th century B.C., tells us that God told Moses exactly what YHWH means:-

> Moses said to God, "Suppose I go to the Israelites and say to them, 'The God of your fathers has sent me to you,' and they ask me, 'What is his name?' Then what shall I tell them?" God said to Moses, "I AM WHO I AM. This is what you are to say to the Israelites: 'I AM has sent me to you.'"

This is a play on the Hebrew verb "to be" HYH. God is saying to Moses, "I am not male or female. I JUST AM." The most holy place for the Jew was the Holy of Holies in the Temple. It contrasted with pagan Near Eastern temples, which would have a statue of either a male or female god as their most holy place. Rather, the great prophet Isaiah has a vision of the Holy of Holies, which scholars date about 740 B.C., where there is no statue, either male or female:-

> "In the year of King Uzziah's death I saw the Lord seated on a high and lofty throne; his train filled the sanctuary. Above him stood seraphs, each one with six wings: two to cover its face, two to cover its feet and two for flying; and they were shouting these words to each other: Holy, holy, holy is Yahweh Sabaoth. His glory fills the whole earth. The door-posts shook at the sound of their shouting, and the Temple was full of smoke. Then I said: 'Woe is me! I am lost, for I am a man of unclean lips and I live among a people of unclean lips, and my eyes have seen the King, Yahweh Sabaoth.'" (*Is* 6:1-5)

Isaiah dare not look at the enthroned YHWH. When the High Priest went into the Holy of Holies once per year, the people prayed that he would be lucky enough to come out alive! If one actually saw YHWH one would die. So God shows only his "back" to Moses when Moses has a vision of YHWH, to save Moses' life.[32]

God said...it happened!

The idea of ritual sex with this Holy God would have been seen as the worst abomination. There is no Shekinah in Isaiah's vision, as Brown makes Professor Langdon tell Sophie, to mate with YHWH. The word Shekinah is never used in the Hebrew Bible. Rather, it was used by the later Rabbis to refer, as O'Collins says, "to the nearness of God to his people, not to some female consort".[33]

In the 8th century B.C., the heyday of the great Hebrew prophets, ritual sex did happen. But the prophet Amos thunders against Israel, where it was practiced, and promises divine punishment:-

> "because they have crushed the heads of the weak into the dust and thrust the rights of the oppressed to one side, father and son sleeping with the same girl and thus profaning my holy name."[34]

Amos, prophesying against the prosperous northern kingdom of Israel, links two crimes together; social injustice and idolatry. The gods of the Canaanites, Baal (male) and Astarte[35] (female) did not bother about the rights of the poor! And, in participating in these pagan rituals, sacred prostitution was involved, "father and son sleeping with the same girl". The Law of Moses strongly condemned ritual prostitution, whether male or female,[36] as "detestable to YHWH your God". So much for sex rites in the Temple involving YHWH and Shekinah!

Why was sacred prostitution so strongly condemned by the Hebrew prophets? It seemed so reasonable to Sophie when Langdon justified Saunière's ritual sex act; "she was starting to understand her grandfather better."[37] The prophets were by no means so sanguine: because for them, it was an offence to the holiness of God, to God's *transcendence*.

Not to say that the Hebrews saw sex as something dirty or reprehensible. Far from it. God created man and woman in his own image, commanding them to increase and multiply.[38] And, in the beautiful story of the creation of the first man and the first woman, the writer of the book of Genesis tells us that by the sex act man and woman become "one flesh"[39] in love.

But YHWH did not have sex, because as God he was above and beyond the world. This did not mean that he had nothing to do with the world. It meant that he was infinitely more powerful than us creatures, as our Creator. "Our God is in heaven: he creates whatever he chooses. They (other nations) have idols of silver and gold, made by human hands. These have mouths but say nothing, have eyes but see nothing...."[40]

This God, the Creator of the world, did not need to have to have sex to make the world. As the book of Genesis says, God simply said, and it happened. "God said, let there be light, and there was light."[41]. For the prophets, it was a serious offence to say that their God YHWH needed a female goddess with whom to mate in order to create the world. God was beyond any need for human activity, or activity with gods, to create.

That was again why the Ten Commandments forbad any image of God,[42] above all in the Temple. Any image would be inadequate to picture the transcendent God. Late on in their history, two hundred years before Christ, faithful Jews died a horrible martyrs death rather than allow "the abomination of desolation",[43] the image of a Greek god, to be placed in the Holy of Holies.

Professor Langdon, however apparently learned, just has no idea.

Mary Magdalene, penitent?

I personally think that all the evidence points to the fact that Gnosticism came early into confrontation with Christianity, as early as the first Christian century. It came particularly with the increasing number of Gentile converts, who were influenced strongly by pagan cults such as the Cult of Mithras, where the believer was literally bathed in the blood of the sacrificed bull.

As we have seen, all the four canonical Gospels are to be dated in the first century A.D. There is no such certain such date for the Gnostic Gospels. They give no solid historical evidence for Jesus, as we shall see the Gospels do. They feed parasitically off the four Gospels, and reinterpret them, in seeing in them a Jesus who can lead the initiate on to higher *gnosis*, a deep and privileged spiritual experience, but not the sacramental life of the Church, the body of Christ.

If we start from this fact, that the Gospels are primary, then the Gnostic texts above concerning Mary Magdalene are easily explained. From the time of Pope Gregory the Great, 591 A.D. onwards,[44] an identification was made between Mary Magdalene and the woman who came to Jesus when he was invited to a meal, and who washed his feet with her tears of penitence and dried his feet with her hair.

Jesus said of this woman that her many sins had been forgiven, for she loved much.[45] This woman is not named in the Gospel of Luke. But an identification with Mary Magdalene was easy enough, even if it was mistaken.

Firstly, it was said of Mary Magdalene that Jesus cast seven devils out of her.[46] It would be easy for an early Christian to see a life of sexual immorality as influenced by the devil, and so for the woman who was a sinner to have been so possessed. Secondly, and even more important, Christ appeared to Mary Magdalene as risen from the dead. Mary is weeping, obviously devastated by the loss of her Rabbi. Jesus appears to her first[47], precisely because she loved him so much; and she loved him so much because she had been forgiven much.

Was this natural identification of Mary Magdalene with the penitent woman only made first by Pope Gregory the Great? Perhaps the Gnostic Gospels themselves are testimony that this interpretation came much earlier. They link implicitly the scene in the Garden where Magdalene meets her beloved Lord with that statement of Jesus that she loved much, like the penitent woman. Again, just as the Church hallows marriage, so by no means does it condemn relationships of love, spiritual friendships which are very deep but not sexual. It is this deep relationship of love with Jesus which is seized upon by the Gnostic Gospels; and even they do not imply that the relationship was sexual. They only say that Jesus returned that special love which Magdalene had for him. They were "companions", "deep friends".

Teabing in The *Da Vinci Code* asserts that branding Mary Magdalene as a prostitute was "a smear campaign launched by the early Church".[48] Again, how little he knows. On the contrary, Pope Gregory's identification of Mary Magdalene with the Penitent Woman elevated her as an icon of penitence. Her life has been an encouragement for all sinners that Jesus accepts them and forgives them if they are penitent. Opposite to being "smeared", Mary Magdalene has been greatly honoured, for instance by an Oxford College being named after her. Students can know that their very sins as with Magdalene can cause them in reaction to love Christ more, as she did.

Since the Second Vatican Council, Mary Magdalene has no longer been called "penitent". Historical study has revealed that there is no clear identification in the Gospels of Mary Magdalene with the Penitent Woman. But I am sure that Mary Magdalene herself, now in heaven, would not have been too concerned that such an identification was made, even if unsubstantiated, if it led sinners to forgiveness, and to greater love of the Saviour.

The God Man

Jesus the Saviour

But this leads us to a deeper question, in fact the most important question arising from The *Da Vinci Code*. We just called Jesus "The Saviour". This title comes from the canonical Gospels. But are they reliable?

The Gospel of Matthew tells us that Joseph, a carpenter from Nazareth, is bothered. He has just betrothed Mary as his wife. But he now finds out that she is pregnant; and not by him! As a faithful Jew, Joseph cannot marry a girl who has already been unfaithful to him. But he does not want to cause shame to the girl, so he is minded to put her away quietly, to cause no scandal in the small town of Nazareth. Matthew goes on:-

> "But after he had considered this, an angel of the Lord appeared to him in a dream and said, 'Joseph son of David, do not be afraid to take Mary home as your wife, because what is conceived in her is from the Holy Spirit. She will give birth to a son, and you are to give him the name Jesus, because he will save his people from their sins.'"[49]

So Jesus is to be the Saviour, born of a young woman Mary who had had no intercourse with a man. This would be a sign of his being the Son of the Most High. As Son of God, He will save his people from their sins.

According to the canonical Gospels, Jesus caused trouble for himself by saying "your sins are forgiven". When he said this to the penitent woman, the bystanders were shocked. "Who is this who forgives sins", they asked.[50] And, when Jesus cured a man lying sick in his bed by saying "Your sins are forgiven", his hearers accused him of blasphemy. Only God can forgive sins, they said.[51]

Even worse, Jesus never denied that he could forgive sins, and do what only God can do. He allowed people to think he had divine power. He made an even more explicit claim to divinity when, at his trial before the Jewish Sanhedrin, the high priest asked him "Are you the Christ, the Son of the living God?" Jesus replied, "I am, and you will see the Son of Man sitting at the right hand of God, and coming in the clouds of heaven."[52] The high priest tore his garments, because he saw that as blasphemy; just as the prophet Isaiah saw as blasphemy the claim of the Assyrian king when he said, "I will climb up to the heavens; and higher than the stars of God I will set my throne."[53]

This was the beginning of the end for Jesus. He was handed over to Pilate, the Roman Governor, and put to death by the "slaves' punishment" of crucifixion, perhaps the cruelest death devised by the evil imagination of the human race.

In a way, we cannot blame those who put him to death. It would have been blasphemy for Jesus to have claimed to be God, had he not been such. Those who put him to death thought that they were acting justly, because they did not accept his claim.

Peter, the leader of the Church, addressed his people the Jews on the Day of Pentecost; fifty days after Jesus had been crucified. He announced that Jesus had risen from the dead. God his Father had vindicated him. They had seen him alive bodily. Peter told them that they could put behind them the fact that, without realizing it, they had put to death the Son of God. Now, he said to his people, "Repent, be baptized, and everyone who calls on the name of the Lord will be saved."[54]

Mary Magdalene, *Saint* Mary Magdalene as the Catholic Church calls her, was identified as we have seen with the penitent woman. She became thereby an icon of the forgiveness of the whole of the human race. According to scripture, the whole of the human race had sinned, from our first parents onwards. This makes us prone to sin, to disobey the commandments of God. We needed a Saviour.

So Christ came. On the night before his betrayal by one of his own disciples Judas, he made a new covenant. At his Last Supper, painted so beautifully by Leonardo da Vinci and by many other artists, he took bread and broke it as a sign of his broken body. He took wine and drank it, as a sign of his poured out blood.[55] He gave it to his disciples to drink as his true body and as his true blood. This was to be their spiritual strength for their journey through this life.[56]

This covenant was "for the remission of sins". Every time his disciples celebrated this new covenant, they made memorial of his death and resurrection, looking forward to Christ's coming again in glory, where they would share in eternal joy with their Saviour. As truly God's Son, sharing his Father's divine nature, he could give us his divine life. As true man, he could share in our sufferings and human joys.

God from God

All this, in The *Da Vinci Code*, is rejected as unhistorical. Teabing announces to the astounded Sophie that Emperor Constantine, for political reasons, engineered the Council of Nicea 325 A.D. to define Jesus as God:-

> "Until that moment in history, Jesus was viewed by His followers as a mortal prophet...a great and powerful man, but a *man* nonetheless. A mortal.
> 'Not the Son of God?' asked Sophie.
> 'Right.' Teabing said."[57]

This is the most incredible nonsense, as any first year theological student would know. At the Council of Nicea, both sides of the debate already accepted that Jesus was the Son of God. The debate was as to what kind of Son of God.

The problem began when a priest called Arius from Alexandria in Egypt began to preach that Jesus was the *created* Son of God. The key passage was in John's Gospel "In the beginning was the Word, and the Word was with God, and the Word was God."[58]

We saw earlier that in the book of Genesis, God created the world simply by his word: "God said, let there be light...and there was light". John, in writing his Gospel, identified this Word of God with Jesus, the eternal Word of God. Arius was influenced by Gnostic thinking, and saw Jesus rather as some kind of emanation from God, but less than God, created and changeable. "There was when he was not", Arius said famously.

Emperor Constantine summoned the Council, but the main influence behind the decisions of the Council was Athanasius, who was to become the champion of orthodoxy as the future Patriarch of Alexandria. The Council taught that Jesus the Word came eternally from God as his eternal and natural Son. As the Nicene Creed says, "God from God, light from light, true God from true God, begotten not made, of one being (*homóousios*) with the Father".

This debate troubled the Church for three centuries, especially with pagan converts coming into the Church who believed in lesser gods, and so tended to support Arianism. The Emperor Constantine was by no means the champion of orthodoxy, as we are told in the *Da Vinci Code*. On the contrary, Constantine tried without success to force Athanasius to accept a compromise formula only three years after the Council![59] As Patriarch, Athanasius was constantly persecuted for holding tenaciously to the faith defined at Nicea.

Christian faith that Jesus was much more than a "mere mortal" was not dreamed up by Constantine. Already, at the beginning of the second century, two hundred years earlier, Pliny the Younger, Roman governor of Pontus/Bithynia from 111-113 AD., wrote to the Emperor Trajan about the Christians. Pliny had found out that they were "accustomed to meet on a fixed day before dawn and sing responsively a hymn to Christ as to a god".[60]

As we have seen, Christian faith is rooted in the story of Jesus as told by the Gospels, which come from the first century of Christianity. Likewise, the Canon of Scripture was not put together by Constantine, as Teabing claims.[61] The Four Gospels were already defined as the only orthodox Gospels by St Irenaeus, who was writing against the Gnostics at the end of the second century A.D.[62]

Finally, Christian worship was not based upon pagan cults, even if it cleverly adopted some practices to help pagan converts make the transition.[63] Rather, its worship was based upon what Jesus handed on, in particular the Last Supper as the most Holy Eucharist. The Eucharist was not celebrated on a Sunday "to coincide with the pagan's veneration day of the sun". [64] Christians before Constantine did not celebrate their liturgy on the Jewish Sabbath, as Langdon says pontifically to the bewildered Sophie.[65]

On the contrary, the 1st century New Testament documents tell us that already two hundred years previously Christians were worshipping on the "Lord's Day", that is the Sunday when Mary Magdalene and the first witnesses saw Christ risen from the dead. This was the "eighth day", the new Sabbath. Christians took only the pagan name-day from the sun god, not their celebration, which on the contrary from the beginning was of the Resurrection of Jesus.

As we have also seen, the Gnostic Gospels date only to A.D.350-400.[66] Why do people then take them seriously when the four canonical Gospels are dated so much earlier? It is all a question of interpretation.

Deconstructing Jesus

Very occasionally, in reading The *Da Vinci Code*, we come across the odd half-truth, to bring us some relief. Teabing, in his long lecture to Sophie about Christian origins, says that, "history is always written by the winners". He quotes Napoleon as saying "What is history, but a fable agreed upon?"[67]

There is just a grain of truth in those remarks. Admittedly, history is not always written by the winners. Diaries are written even by prisoners in concentration camps. And history is not always either a fable agreed upon. That would be much too cynical. There are many important facts communicated in history books and in historical documents.

But Teabing is right in that history is not an exact science. In this scientific age, we tend to think that every truth must be contained in a test tube or in a mathematical formula. But "history" cannot be tested in a laboratory. History is written by human beings, and we have to make a *judgement of faith* in what has been recorded. We have to believe the human witnesses, whether we are dealing with documents about the Battle of Hastings, or the death certificate of your great-grandmother.

In fact, in my recent book about the historicity of the Gospels, I produced the following formula as to what constitutes the origin of an "historical fact":-

"X told me that Y really happened. I believe X."[68]

Every so-called "historical fact" is simply an event the account of which I accept as authentic, believing a witness or witnesses of it. Historical science is more like an interrogation in a courtroom than a dissection in a path. lab. Is the witness credible? Or is he or she lying? Or is he or she deceived?

In terms strictly of historical investigation, the Gospels could be by eye-witnesses. They could be true accounts. As we have seen, they were written at the latest at the end of the first century or the beginning of the second.[69] But are they to be believed? That is the two thousand year old question. If their authors were deceived or deceivers, then it matters nothing if they were produced in the newspaper the day after the Feeding of the Five Thousand, or the Monday morning after Mary Magdalene found the tomb of Jesus empty and met the risen Jesus in the Garden.

In the past two hundred years, the "Quest of the Historical Jesus" has generally been about deconstructing Jesus, to bring him to a point of post-Enlightenment credibility. We did not have to wait for Dan Brown to say that Jesus was not God, and that the miracles of Jesus justifying his divinity are not to be believed. In 1780, a Hamburg philologist called Reimarus claimed that the historical Jesus never claimed to be God, but tried unsuccessfully to start a revolution. Jesus was crucified, and his disciples spread the myth of his resurrection in order to get themselves a better career than fishing!

Two hundred years later, little has changed. The *Jesus Seminar*, a group of American academics, came together in the early 1990s and dropped coloured beads into a box to signify whether this or that verse in the Gospels was authentically by Jesus.[70] Like Reimarus, they came to the conclusion that Jesus never claimed to be God, but was a Jewish prophet elevated by the Christian Church to the status of a God, to bolster its authority.

My contention is that both Reimarus a long time ago and The *Jesus Seminar* most recently did not prove their case at all. They assumed it from the beginning. They did not accept even as a hypothesis that God could become man. They did not accept the possibility of the miracles of Jesus which proved his divinity. Small wonder therefore that their "historical Jesus" was a considerably reduced figure from the Christ proclaimed in the Gospels!

Many Christian scholars who are believers have followed this reductionist line. They have made a distinction between the "Jesus of history" and "the Christ of faith". They argue that historically we can only prove that Jesus was an "eschatological prophet"; a prophet who came to announce the last times when God would save the whole world. They still believe the Nicene Creed; but they have to make that an act of pure faith.

I believe that we can do better. We have on the contrary good historical foundations for incarnational faith. But we must begin at the beginning.

The critical minimum

One good effect of the enormous amount of research into the historical Jesus over the past two hundred years is that scholars have come to some kind of consensus, which is often called "the Critical Minimum", as to facts about Jesus which scholars find credible, even if they are not Christian believers.

Firstly, there is no doubt that a person called Jesus of Nazareth existed, and that he was the founder of the

Christian religion. This we can confirm by contemporary historical witnesses hostile or at least indifferent to Christianity. The most important Roman witness to Jesus' existence is the historian Tacitus, (A.D. 55-120)[71] who, writing his Roman annals between A.D. 115 and 117, mentions the Great Fire of Rome in A.D. 64 and Nero's attempt to fasten the blame for it on the Christians. This is obviously very important evidence of the existence of Jesus, since clearly Tacitus is not biased in favour of Christianity, and wrote his annals as an historical account less than a hundred years after the death of Jesus.

Other important witnesses to the existence of Jesus are Josephus, a Jewish historian who wrote at the time of the Jewish war against the Romans, A.D. 70., Mara Bar Sapion, a Syrian Stoic who lived in the very area where Jesus practiced his ministry[72]; and the Jewish Talmud, which, while saying that Jesus was put to death "for sorcery", assumes that he existed[73]. Surely, Jesus' own people would have known if he had not existed!

As Theissen/Merz in their book *The Historical Jesus: A Comprehensive Guide* say correctly, "both opponents and neutral or sympathetic observers of Christianity presuppose the historicity of Jesus and do not indicate a shadow of doubt about it".[74] Neither should we.

But scholars do not only affirm without serious question now that Jesus existed. They have reached a "Critical Minimum" about what the historical Jesus said and did from the use of criteria of credibility; again, the same kind of criteria that a defending lawyer might use to test the truth of a witness' testimony in court.

The Gospels tell us that Jesus came to preach the "kingdom of God", which indeed he saw as coming about by his own casting out of demons[75]. This is quite a unique message. No prophet before Jesus had claimed that the kingdom of God would actually come about by his miracles. And the first Christians did not use the phrase "kingdom of God" to describe Jesus' work on earth. Scholars conclude therefore that there is what they call a "double discontinuity" here. Jesus preaching the kingdom of God as coming with his own life and ministry is discontinuous with his past and with the future, and is therefore authenticated historically.

Using similar criteria as well as that of double discontinuity to authenticate words and events in Jesus' life[76], scholars agree that Jesus was renowned in his time as a miracle worker; that he came from Nazareth, and began his ministry in Galilee, north of Judea; that his ministry was linked with that of John the Baptist, summoning Israel to repentance; that he became unpopular with the Jewish authorities because of his criticism of Rabbinic laws, and because of his association with outcasts and sinners, who were considered by strict Pharisaism untouchables; and that, some time between 26-36 A.D., he went up to Jerusalem and was arrested, being put to death by the Roman governor Pontius Pilate[77].

But the "critical minimum", while most useful for presenting to us well authenticated facts concerning the life, ministry, and death of Jesus, does not answer three fundamental questions about him. First, why did the Christian community come to invest so much faith in Jesus as the Son of God? Secondly, why was Jesus eventually put to death? And thirdly, why was the Christian Church so phenomenally successful from its beginning? I argue in my book *Bad, Mad, or God? Proving the Divinity of Christ from St John's Gospel*, that these answers can only be given from the Gospels themselves; but only if we open our minds to the possibility of the truth of the Gospels, that is the possibility of miracles, and of God becoming man for us. In other words, we must remove our post-Enlightenment blinkers.

Bad, mad or God?

In Britain, just after the Second World War 1939-45, many people were drifting away from Christian faith. C. S. Lewis, a great man of letters, author of the *Narnia* books, came to believe in what he called *Mere Christianity*. He became a most successful writer and broadcaster in defence of the traditional faith of this country.

What persuaded him about the truth of Christian faith was the following argument, which he called "Bad, Mad or God?" Jesus claimed to be God Lewis said... If he did so claim, you could not conclude that he was just a good man. If he made such a stupendous claim, he had either to be bad, a deceiver; or he had to be mad, like those unfortunate patients in a psychiatric hospital who have delusions of grandeur.

But, argues Lewis, the Gospels show us a man who is neither bad nor mad. On the contrary, all agree that Jesus of Nazareth was wise and sane. Furthermore, Lewis said, if God wished to give us a revelation to believe, a God become man, that person would have to do mighty deeds to prove his credentials; like walk on the water and feed five thousand people with five loaves and two fishes; as well as being morally good. This is precisely what we find in the Gospel accounts.

After a lifetime's study of the four Gospels, I buy into that argument. The Gospels are not tape-recordings of Jesus' life. They do not often contain the actual words he said (the *ipsissima verba*). The Catholic Church never requires us to believe that.[78] Sometimes the Gospels give us the reported speech of Jesus. But the Gospels contain substantially what Jesus said and did. A recent study has shown that the Gospels are in the form of a classical biography, where history is important.[79] And what the Gospels say is credible, if we, unlike Reimarus and the *Jesus Seminar* at least allow ourselves the possibility at first to believe that it might be true. They make sense.

More and more scholars are admitting the Jewish nature of the Gospels. In the 19th century, the stock opinion was that St Paul elevated the Jewish prophet Jesus to become a Hellenistic God. This led eventually to the Fourth Gospel, purported to be by John, where Greek philosophy comes to fruition with Jesus presented as the Logos.

John in the Fourth Gospel presents a clear historical argument. He claims that Jesus claimed to be God, and substantiated that claim:-

- The miracles of Jesus, particularly the Walking on the Water and the Multiplication of the Loaves, demonstrated to the disciples, at least as they understood it after the Resurrection, that he was the manifestation of the divine logos.
- Jesus was fully aware of his own divine nature, and proclaimed it explicitly in the Temple courtyard just prior to his arrest, identifying himself with the YHWH God of the old Testament, the I AM, a claim which was seen as blasphemous by many of his hearers.
- It was first and foremost because of these claims that Jesus was arrested and then handed over to Pontius Pilate the Roman Governor.
- Jesus made these claims in the Jerusalem Temple courtyard because he believed that "the Jews", that is those of God's chosen people who had the privilege of living in Jerusalem and Judea, had the right of hearing the message of salvation and of forming the renewed people of God following Jesus "the light of the world".

- Jesus after his death appeared bodily to the women and his disciples, who discovered his tomb empty. This demonstrated to the apostles that Jesus was precisely whom he claimed to be during his life, the Word become flesh, fully worthy of doubting Thomas' worshipful proclamation "My Lord and my God". [*John* 20:28]
- Thus all the readers of the Fourth Gospel are invited to share in the faith of once doubting Thomas.

The discoveries at Qumran, on the shores of the Dead Sea, have more and more demonstrated the Jewishness of John, and authenticate the early date of the Gospels. Once more, our English aristocrat Teabing has got it wrong. He says, again lecturing Sophie, "Dead Sea Scrolls...do not match up with the gospels in the Bible.[80]" You would hardly expect them to, since the monks at Qumran were not Christians!

However, the scholarly view now is that the scrolls found in caves on the shores of the Dead Sea by a Bedouin in 1947 confirm the first century dating of the four canonical Gospels. Ideas which in the 19th century were said to prove the Hellenistic origin of John's ideas, such as his contrast between darkness and light [1:4-5,9], Jesus as the truth [14:6], and the Spirit of Truth [14:17,26], are present in the documents of the 1st century A.D in Judea and are thoroughly Semitic.[81] The Gospel of John in particular presents a Jewish Jesus.

This is above all true of Chapters 7-10 of John, where Jesus enters Jerusalem for the last time, and stakes his claim before his own people. He claims full divinity, but in a thoroughly Jewish way. "Before Abraham was, I AM".[82] This recalls the Exodus story which we have already quoted, where God reveals himself to Moses as YHWH. In Greek, that is *egó eimi*, I AM. Jesus is revealing himself to his people as their divine redeemer. Later he says to his astounded Jewish hearers, "I and the Father are One".[83] Jesus is not denying the unity of God, asserted in the Jewish *shema'*, "Hear, O Israel, the Lord our God is one Lord". On the contrary, Jesus is saying that his Godhead is one with the Godhead of his Father, as the Word comes forth from God and is God.

Jesus is accused of blasphemy, and eventually is crucified. But he rises again from the dead and, after two thousand years, his believers amount to billions. Elaine Pagels, at the end of a book where she shows great sympathy for Gnosticism, has to admit:-

> "...the religious perspectives and methods of Gnosticism did not lend themselves to mass religion. In this respect, it was no match for the highly effective system of organization of the catholic church, which expressed a unified religious perspective based on the New Testament canon, offered a creed requiring the initiate to confess only the simplest essentials of faith,

and celebrated rituals as simple and profound as baptism and the eucharist."[84]

That is as true today as it was in the first, second and third Christian centuries when the Church was competing with Gnosticism. It is just as true today when our competing philosophies are secularism and new age rituals. The reason, of course, is not just organization, nor even simplicity. It is that God has given a revelation, and he has been successful in imparting it. You would expect nothing less from the Creator of the universe! It was meant for everyone, for "the masses", and the masses recognize it.

To see my argument more in detail, you will have to read my book *Bad, Mad or God?* But we must now conclude this short pamphlet, asking ourselves one last question. How on earth has Dan Brown been so successful with The *Da Vinci Code*? Most of us authors struggle to sell thousands, even hundreds, of our books. Why is The *Da Vinci Code* such a phenomenal success? The answer to that question tells us something about the general state of religion in our Western culture at the beginning of the third millennium.

The Da Vinci distraction

I once heard of a crowd gathering in central London. But they were all conned. A man was pointing up to the top of a building, and looking up there. Within a few minutes, a crowd had gathered, looking up at the top of the building with him. There was nothing there to see, except the top of the building.

That is a good parable of the *Da Vinci Code*. As I said earlier, the book is a tease. It sets people on to a wild goose chase which will never come to any conclusion. Meanwhile, the author and the publishers make a killing, as do the tour companies arranging visits to the Louvre and to the Rosslyn Chapel.

We do not wish to deny anyone any fun, or for that matter a fortune. But there is a more serious matter at stake here. At the beginning of the twentieth century, many people thought that religion would not survive the next hundred years. Their views would have been confirmed by the huge spread of atheistic Communism, which by the sixties was ruling the whole of the Eastern half of the world. At the same time, the practice of religion was declining in the West.

But at the beginning of the new millennium, people perhaps are not quite so sure. God perhaps is not dead after all. Rather, atheistic totalitarianism is dead. Communism just collapsed from within. The myth just exploded. The practice of religion is growing throughout the world, apart from in the secular West. Even here in Britain, some say the most irreligious country in the world, the death of Pope John Paul II aroused huge media interest. It does seem that people are beginning to find secularism clapped out, and are searching for something more. As the *Catechism of the Catholic Church* tells us, the desire for God is written in every human heart.[85] As Augustine said centuries ago, addressing God, "our heart is restless until it rests in you".[86]

In flitting around trying to crack the *Da Vinci Code*, people are distracted from the genuine search for God. The *Da Vinci Code* is an easy option. It gives reasons, however absurd, for rejecting the Christian faith people were taught at school and at home. The *Da Vinci Code* is a gift to the confused post-Christian mind of the twenty-first century. It offers the Christian story without pain, without effort and without commitment. It anaesthetises the Jesus story. It saves people the pain of making a decision which might change their lives. It was not easy for the Prodigal Son to return home to his father. It was not easy for the Penitent Woman - whether or not she was Mary Magdalene - to endure the shame of entering the dining room to wash Jesus' feet.

Conclusion

The Church I love

Reading The *Da Vinci Code* for me has been a pain. I have been commissioned to write this pamphlet, to present the true story of Jesus, and to refute a few of the major historical errors of this novel. But it was by no means an enjoyable experience, even though I admire the writing skills of Dan Brown. I am a priest of the Catholic Church, and I love the Catholic Church. I feel some anger that the Church, my spiritual mother, is being constantly undermined and vilified unjustly throughout The *Da Vinci Code.*

Of course, it is not only the authenticity of the present day Roman Catholic Church which comes under fire in this novel. In attempting to rubbish the doctrine of the divinity of Christ defined at the Council of Nicea, Brown attacks all the main line Christian denominations. The Council of Nicea came long before the Christian divisions; the Orthodox not separating from Rome until the beginning of the second millennium; while the Protestant groups did not break away from the unity of Rome until the sixteenth century, twelve hundred years after Nicea. These denominations accept both the orthodox Canon of the New Testament and the doctrine of the divinity of Christ.

But our author saves his prime invective for the present day Catholic Church and for one part of it in particular. The villain of the novel is the murderer, a "hulking albino"[87] called Silas. He is a member of *Opus Dei* which is a personal Prelature of the Catholic Church that helps ordinary lay people seek holiness in their work and everyday activities. Silas wears "the spiked *cilice* belt clamped around his thigh". "All true followers of *The Way* wore this device - a leather strap, studded with sharp metal barbs that cut into the flesh as a perpetual reminder of Christ's suffering".[88] Silas lashes himself with the *Discipline*, a "heavy knotted rope"[89] called the discipline.

It is true that Opus Dei "has just completed construction of a $47 million National Headquarters at 243 Lexington Avenue in New York City".[90] But it is worth noting that this would seem to be a relatively moderate price to pay today for a building for the headquarters of a large organization in New York.

Opus Dei has been attributed with a reputation for secrecy, deserved or undeserved, and it is true that there is some entirely voluntary and strictly limited use of the cilice and the discipline (a whip used for self-chastisement), both of these are traditional means in Christianity for ascetism. But it would be entirely wrong, indeed sinful, in the Catholic Church, for such chastisement to cause physical wounding to oneself, or to be used with the motivation of masochism.

This evil characterization of Opus Dei must be very hurtful to the thousands of members of Opus Dei worldwide... They are not monks, as depicted in the *Da Vinci Code*. They are lay people in all levels of society, trying to live their Christian vocation in the world. They do not need this twisted portrayal.

Brown also continually blackens the Church's role in history. I have tried to deal with a few of these misrepresentations of the facts. But I must deal finally with Professor Langdon's incredible statement to Sophie when he says, "During three hundred years of witch hunts, The Church burned at the stake five *million* women".[91] O'Collins comments:-

> "The killing of alleged witches was a horrible crime in the story of Christianity. But the idea that the Catholic Church burned at the stake five million women is bizarre. That kind of savagery would have depopulated Europe. Experts give instead the statistic of around 50,000 victims for the three centuries of witch hunts carried out by Catholics and Protestants in Northern Europe and elsewhere. Around 20% of the victims were men, and not all alleged witches died by being burnt at the stake. But it suits Brown to multiply the figure by one hundred, and come up with five million women burned by the Catholic Church."[92]

In an organization with more than a billion members worldwide, the Church will always present a tarnished image, because it has imperfect members. The Catholic Church is not the church of the perfect. Jesus said, "I have not come to call the righteous, but sinners to repentance".[93] We are a Church of sinners, each of us trying to change with the help Jesus has given us with his Holy Spirit in the Church his body.

This image has been especially tarnished in our own time with the much publicized abuse cases, which, although totally reprehensible, constitute a minute proportion of priests and nuns. These were not sins only. They were crimes. But it would be totally unfair to blacken the character of the whole Church because of the crimes of a relative few. No one would blame the police force or carers in nursing homes en block for a tiny minority of sexual abusers who somehow managed to infiltrate their profession.

For its part, The *Da Vinci Code* gives an entirely unjust and negative view of the actual Catholic Church, from persistent accusations in its history, as we have seen, most without foundation, and the rest exaggerated. It does not mention that the Catholic Church is the biggest education and health provider in the world. It does not mention that its government bureaucracy, represented in the novel by scheming and overweight bishops, is the lowest paid and yet one of the most efficient organizations in the world. It does not mention saints like Francis of Assisi and Mother Teresa of Calcutta who are human beings the quality of which you will meet nowhere else than in the Church. It does not mention the spiritual comfort and help given in the confessional by nearly half a million priests worldwide, its confidentiality the most carefully protected of any professional organization.

Above all, it is not the Church I have known intimately for most of my adult life. The image of the Catholic Church I have is a personal and very simple one. When a young teenage boy, I used to deliver groceries deposited in a small wheelbarrow to the local convent, from the grocery store owned by my widowed mother. I would push the wheelbarrow up the Charlton Road, and deliver the groceries to kind and smiling nuns, receiving the tip of a sixpence; not bad value in those days!

Later, when I was received into full communion with the Catholic Church, I learnt that the private primary school they ran was very popular among the working class community of the Charlton Estate. Often, the people said, if the sisters knew a family was running into hard times, they would "forget" to charge them their school fees. In any case, the fees were affordable for those on low incomes, because the sisters had taken a vow of poverty, and the cost of maintaining the teaching staff was a fraction of what it would be in a lay school.

I am glad that the Church found a place for me, as it will find a place for anyone who believes and is baptised. The Catholic Church is no secret organization, but issues an open invitation to all to share the life of God in its sacramental life. I have found in the Church the love of Christ and the inspiration of good people to keep me faithful. Recently, the BBC put out a series of television programmes led by a group of professionals who were studying the science of how to make people happy! I have found that happiness in the Church which I know and love. I do hope that this little pamphlet will lead people to turn from having read the *Da Vinci Code* to reading the uncoded versions of Matthew, Mark, Luke and John. I hope and pray that there they will find the spiritual truth and happiness which God coming to earth as a man called Jesus came to give them.

Endnotes

[1] *Mt* 27:56, 61; 28:1; *Mk* 15:40, 47; 16:1, 9; *Lk* 24:10; *Jn* 19:25; 20:1, 18
[2] *Lk* 8:2.
[3] http://news.nationalgeographic.com/news/2004/12/1217_041217_tv_da vinci_code.html
[4] *Jn* 20:1-18.
[5] *Mt* 8:14
[6] 1 *Cor* 7:32.
[7] *Mt* 8:20, *Lk* 9:58.
[8] *Mk* 14:64.
[9] *Lk* 18:33.
[10] *Mt* 19:12
[11] *Mk* 3:35
[12] Brown, p.333.
[13] Article on the Metareligion website: "to promote a multidisciplinary view of the religious, spiritual and esoteric phenomena". http://www.metareligion.com/World_Religions/Christianity/Other_Books/Nag_Hammadi/nag_hammadi_library.htm
[14] *The Son of God and the Son of Man: the Macro and Micro Cosmic Principles of the Cosmic Christ. The Docetic Vision.* http://www.vermontel.com/~vt sophia/sonofgod.htm.
[15] 1 *Jn* 4:2
[16] Brown, p.331.
[17] Brown, p.331.
[18] *The History of the Coptic Language*, http://www.stshenouda.com/coptlang/copthist.htm#OrginChristians
[19] Olson and Miesel, p.94.
[20] Leloup, Y-V., *The Gospel of Mary Magdalene, Translation from the Coptic and Commentary*, English Translation and Notes by J.Rowe. Vermont, Inner Traditions International, 2002, pp.10-11
[21] Pagels, E. *The Gnostic Gospels*, London, Penguin Books, 1990, p.84.
[22] Olson and Miesel, p.95.
[23] Brown, p.333
[24] *Jn* 21:17.
[25] *Jn* 13:23.
[26] Cf. Olson and Miesel, p.181.
[27] Brown, p.584.
[28] Brown, p.593.
[29] Brown, p.411.
[30] Brown, p.411.
[31] *Ex* 3:1
[32] *Ex* 30:20-23
[33] O'Collins, p.72.

[34] *Am* 2:7

[35] A female goddess mentioned in 1*K* 11:5 as "the goddess of the Sidonians".

[36] *Dt* 23:18-19

[37] Brown, p.412.

[38] *Gn* 1:27.

[39] *Gn* 2:24.

[40] *Ps* 115:3-5

[41] *Gn* 1:3.

[42] *Ex* 20:4, *Dt* 5:8.

[43] *Dn* 11:31.

[44] Olson and Miesel, p.82.

[45] *Lk* 7:47.

[46] *Mk* 16:9.

[47] *Jn* 20:1-18

[48] Brown, p.328.

[49] *Mt* 2:20-21.

[50] *Lk* 7:49.

[51] *Mk* 2:7.

[52] *Mk* 14:62.

[53] *Is* 14:13

[54] *Ac* 2:21.

[55] *Mt* 26:26-27

[56] *Jn* 6:54.

[57] Brown, p.315.

[58] *Jn* 1:1

[59] Catholic Encylopaedia, article *Arius*, http.//ww.newadvent.org/cathen01718a.htm.

[60] http://ccat.sas.upenn.edu/jod/texts/pliny.html

[61] Brown, p.313.

[62] Wickenhauser, A. *New Testament Introduction*. New York, Herder and Herder, 1958, p.38.

[63] Brown, p.314.

[64] Brown, pp.314-315.

[65] Brown, pp.314-315, cf. Olson and Miesel, p.159. *Ac* 20:7, *Rv* 1:10.

[66] Article on the Metareligion website: "to promote a multidisciplinary view of the religious, spiritual and esoteric phenomena". http://www.metareligion.com/World_Religions/Christianity/Other_Books/Nag_Hammadi/nag_hammadi_library.htm

[67] Brown, p.343.

[68] Redford, J. *Bad, Mad, or God? Proving the Divinity of Christ from St John's Gospel*. London, St Paul's Publishing, 2004, P.84.

[69] Re Matthew, Mark and Luke, cf. Redford, p.78. Regarding John cf. Redford, cf.Redford, p.160.

[70] Funk, R.W. Hoover, R.W., and The Jesus Seminar, *The Five Gospels: The Search for the Authentic Words of Jesus*. New York, Scribner, 1993.

[71] Redford, p.106.

[72] Redford, p.109.

[73] Redford, p.110.

[74] Theissen G., and Merz.,A., *The Historical Jesus: A Comprehensive Guide*, London, SCM, 1998.

[75] *Lk* 11:19-20.

[76] Redford, pp.118-120.

[77] Redford, pp.118-120.

[78] C. the *Instruction of the Pontifical Biblical Commission Concerning the Historical Truth of the Gospels*, 21 April, 1964.

[79] Burridge, R.A. *What Are the Gospels? A Comparison with Graeco-Roman Biography*. Society for New Testament Studies. Monograph Series, 70. Cambridg University Press, 1992

[80] Brown, p.331.

[81] Redford, p.162.

[82] *Jn* 8:58.

[83] *Jn* 10:30.

[84] Pagels, p.146.

[85] *CCC* 27.

[86] *CCC* 30, quoting Augustine, *Confessions*, 1,1,1: PL 32.

[87] Brown, p.27.

[88] Brown, p.29.

[89] Brown, p.30

[90] Brown, p.15.

[91] Brown, p.173.

[92] O'Collins, p.74.

[93] *Mt* 9:13